Wolves

Laura Marsh

SCHOLASTIC INC.

For Bonnie

—L. F. M.

All wolves pictured are gray wolves, unless otherwise noted.

ISBN 978-0-545-54860-1

18 17 16 15 14 13 16 17/0

Printed in the U.S.A. 40

First Scholastic printing, December 2012

Design by YAY! Design

Cover, Altrendo Nature/Altrendo RR/Getty Images; 1, Lynn M. Stone/Kimball Stock; 2, Tom Leeson/NationalGeographicStock.com; 4–5, Digital Vision; 6, Jim Brandenburg/NationalGeographicStock.com; 7 (top), Wildlife GmbH/www.kimballstock.com; 7 (center), Zerlina Chen/Your Shot/NationalGeographicStock.com; 7 (bottom), Ana Gram/Shutterstock; 8 (A), Eric Isselée/iStockphoto.com; 8 (B), Joel Sartore/NationalGeographicStock.com; 8 (C), Roy Toft/NationalGeographicStock.com; 8 (D), Ann and Steve Toon/Robert Harding/Getty Images; 8 (E), lifeonwhite.com/iStockphoto.com; 8 (bottom), Valerii Kaliuzhnyi/iStockphoto.com; 9 (left), Stanisław Pytel/iStockphoto.com; 9 (right), Joseph Van Os/The Image Bank/Getty Images; 10 (top), Kimball Stock; 10 (bottom), Lisa A. Svara/Shutterstock; 12–13, E. A. Janes/SuperStock; 14–15, Joel Sartore/NationalGeographicStock.com; 17, Corbis Flirt/Alamy; 19, Jacqueline Crivello/Your Shot/NationalGeographicStock.com; 20–21, John Pitcher/iStockphoto.com; 20, Jim Brandenburg/Minden Pictures; 22, Robert Harding World Imagery/Getty Images; 23, Picture Press/Alamy; 24 (top left), First Light/Getty Images; 24 (top right), Fedor Kondratenko/iStockphoto.com; 24 (bottom left), iStockphoto.com; 24 (bottom right), Images in the Wild/iStockphoto.com; 25 (top left), Dario Egidi/iStockphoto.com; 25 (top right), Jim Brandenburg/Minden Pictures; 25 (bottom left), Marcia Straub/iStockphoto.com; 25 (bottom right), Digital Vision; 26, Rolf Hicker/photolibrary.com; 27, Jean-Edouard Rozey/Shutterstock; 28–29, Joel Sartore/NationalGeographicStock.com; 30 (top), Galyna Andrushko/Shutterstock; 30 (center), Tammy Wolfe/iStockphoto.com; 30 (bottom), J-E ROZEY/iStockphoto.com; 31 (top left), Paolo Capelli/National Geographic My Shot/NationalGeographicStock.com; 31 (top right), Joel Sartore/NationalGeographicStock.com; 31 (bottom left), Acilo/iStockphoto.com; 31 (bottom right), Marek Brzezinski/iStockphoto.com; 32 (top left), Jacqueline Crivello/Your Shot/ NationalGeographicStock.com; 32 (top right), Jim Brandenburg/Minden Pictures; 32 (left center), Stanisław Pytel/iStockphoto.com; 32 (right center), Franco Tempesta; 32 (bottom left), Design Pics Inc./Alamy; 32 (bottom right), Jeff Lepore/Photo Researchers, Inc.

Table of Contents

What's That Sound?

Arrooooooo!

There's a lonely howl in the distance. Then more voices join in. The chorus of howls sends a shiver down your spine.

What's making this spooky sound?

Wolves!

Wolves All Around

Wolves are found all over the world. They live in hot places like deserts. They also live in cold places like the North Pole.

The most common wolf is the gray wolf.

There are more than 30 kinds of gray wolves. And they are not just gray. They are brown, black, tan, and white, too.

Three Kinds of Gray Wolves

Iberian Wolf

Arctic Wolf

Timber Wolf

Wolves and Dogs

Wolves are the largest members of the dog family. Foxes, coyotes, jackals, wild dogs, and domestic dogs are also members of this family.

German Shepherd

Timber Wolf

Our pet dogs are relatives of the gray wolf. That's why they look alike.

Word bite

DOMESTIC: Tame and kept by humans

This wolf and Golden Retriever are cousins!
Wolf
longer snout
stronger jaws
larger teeth
Dog
rounder head
shorter legs

Q What did the wolf say to his friend?

A Howl's it going?

But wolves and dogs are different in several ways.

Wolves have a longer snout, stronger jaws, and larger teeth. Dogs have a rounder head and shorter legs.

The biggest difference is that dogs like to be around people, and wolves would rather be around other wolves.

Pack Life

Wolves live in family groups called packs. A pack includes a male and female wolf, their young, and a few wolves that have joined from other packs.

There are usually six to ten wolves in a pack.

Wolves need each other. Together they find food, protect one another, and care for their young. A wolf alone can't survive for long.

Hunting

Wolves are great hunters. They travel many miles without getting tired. They can usually run faster than their prey.

Wolves eat small animals such as rabbits. They also eat big animals such as moose, deer, caribou, elk, and bison.

And wolves eat a lot. They can each eat 20 pounds of meat in one meal. That's about 200 hot dogs!

Word bite

PREY: An animal that is eaten by another animal

Wolf Talk

How do wolves "talk" to the other wolves in their pack? They whimper, bark, growl, and snarl.

But when they need to talk long distance, wolves howl. And when one wolf starts howling, others tend to join in.

Howling is what wolves are famous for!

Watch out!
Help!
Where are you?
Yippee! We caught dinner!
Come hunting with me!
Stay off my turf!

Leaders of the Pack

The pack's leaders are called alpha wolves. There is one alpha male and one alpha female in each pack. They are the smartest and best hunters.

Alpha wolves guide the pack. They decide when to stop hunting and where to sleep at night. Alpha wolves also eat first at every meal.

Word bite

ALPHA: A leader in a group

An alpha wolf lays its nose on top of a pack member's nose to show who's boss.

Pups

Baby wolves are called pups. Four to six pups are usually born in each litter.

Pups weigh one pound at birth and can't see or hear. They snuggle safely in their den with their mother for the first two weeks.

Every day they grow bigger and stronger. At about three weeks old, the pups leave the den to explore.

Word bite

LITTER: A group of animals born at one time

DEN: A hidden place in a cave or underground where animals live

When the pups are bigger, other wolves in the pack care for them, too. They bring the pups food. They also babysit them while the rest of the pack is hunting.

Q What do you call a lost wolf?

A A where-wolf!

Wolf pups start hunting with the pack when they are six months old. When young wolves are two to three years old, they leave to form their own packs.

8 Wolf Wonders

1

Pups open their eyes when they are about two weeks old.

2

A wolf's sense of smell is about 100 times greater than a human's sense of smell.

3

Newborn pups can't keep themselves warm. They need mom for body heat.

4

Each wolf has its own howl, which sounds different from the howl of other wolves.

Q How do wolves eat?

A They wolf down their food!

5

Wolves usually won't hunt outside their own hunting grounds.

6

Pups play with "toys" such as a small dead animal from a kill, or a piece of its bone or fur.

7

An alpha wolf shows who's boss by walking tall with its tail and ears held high.

8

Wolves roam long distances – as far as 12 miles in one day!

Fewer Wolves

Wolves rarely attack people. They are afraid of them. But wolves do attack farm animals. Mostly for this reason, people have killed millions of wolves. So many wolves were killed that there were no longer any wolves in a lot of places.

Furs of wolves killed by hunters

Today there are about 100 red wolves living in the wild.

Some people worried that wolves might become extinct. So they decided to help.

They passed laws to protect wolves. Today wolves are returning to many places around the world.

Word bite

EXTINCT: A group of animals no longer living

Wolves Return

Wolves have returned to Yellowstone National Park. Once the park had many wolves. But only one wolf was left by 1926.

Q Why did the wolf want the chicken to join the band?

A He wanted drumsticks!

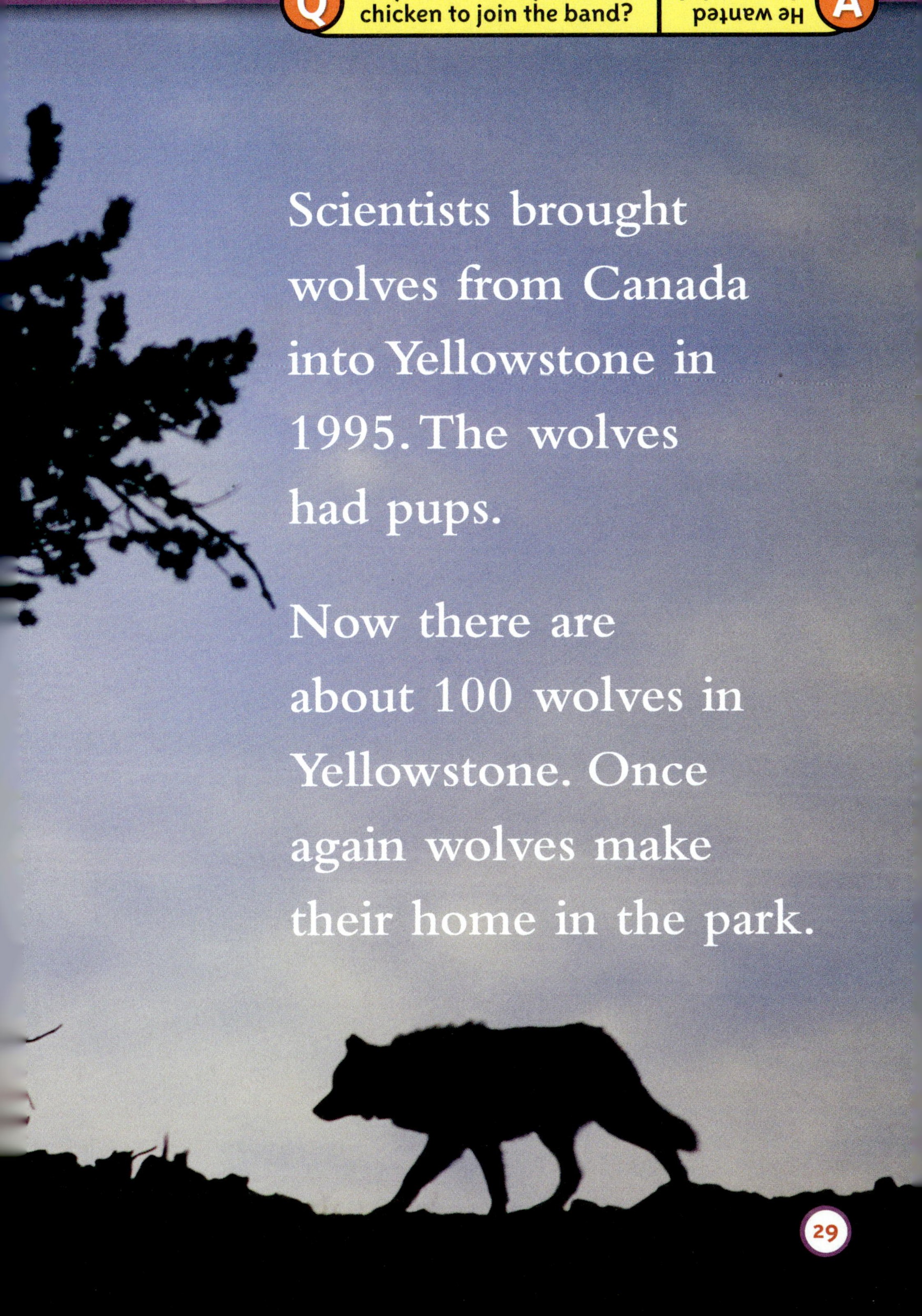

Scientists brought wolves from Canada into Yellowstone in 1995. The wolves had pups.

Now there are about 100 wolves in Yellowstone. Once again wolves make their home in the park.

Stump Your Parents

Can your parents answer these questions about wolves? You might know more than they do!

Answers at bottom of page 31.

1

Where do wolves live?

A. In the desert
B. In the mountains
C. In the forest
D. All of the above

2

Wolves like to "talk" long distance to one another by ________.

A. Chirping
B. Squealing
C. Howling
D. Buzzing

3

What is the most common kind of wolf?

A. Red wolf
B. Gray wolf
C. Italian wolf
D. Werewolf

4

What is the leader of a wolf group called?

A. Head wolf
B. President
C. Alpha wolf
D. Chief

5

What is a baby wolf called?

A. A cub
B. A calf
C. A pup
D. A foal

6

What is the main reason there are fewer wolves today?

A. Hunters
B. Pollution
C. Hurricanes
D. Disease

7

What do wolves like to eat?

A. Hamburgers and french fries
B. Berries and grasses
C. Insects
D. Rabbits, deer, and elk

Answers: 1) D, 2) C, 3) B, 4) C, 5) C, 6) A, 7) D

ALPHA: A leader in a group

DEN: A hidden place in a cave or underground where animals live

DOMESTIC: Tame and kept by humans

EXTINCT: A group of animals no longer living

LITTER: A group of animals born at one time

PREY: An animal that is eaten by another animal